Another Raw Collection

Anthony Luta

BookLeaf
Publishing

India | USA | UK

Presentation by *BookLeaf Publishing*

Web: www.bookleafpub.com

E-mail: info@bookleafpub.com

ISBN: 9789357447416

First edition 2022

DEDICATION

I dedicate this collection to my boyfriend Nate
for always being there for me when I need him.

And to my mother for always believing in
whatever I venture in next.

Dreaded Muse

When pain is gone,
And anger fades,
Cries an absence,
Left in whispers.

Stories of greats,
Fallen to excess,
Begs the question,
Where's the muse,

When the muse is numb.

Or are you deaf?

Gliding Keys

The saying goes,
"Practice makes perfect,"
So jump back on,
The bike you lost.

It may be trash,
Or something good,
You never know,
Until you show.

Taxes

Why fear the man,
Who holds the strings,
You try to cut,
On future's wings.

So take the leap,
You'll find the key,
Of joy awaits,
On calmer seas.

A Golden Drop

The spark of life,
Itself contained,
To lead through strife,
Or kept maintained.

Energy lives,
Morning or night,
To pass through sieves,
And fight the blight.

Off

Doors close,
Windows open,
Sometimes you jump,
Without a 'chute.

Your brain screams,
You have to run,
But where to go?
That's half the fun.

Windows Open

The cards did say,
Pharm would drag me,
From my other half,
Lover or craft.

And now I see,
Open windows,
Carry in the word,
Of muses lost.

Missing

A chill rolls through,
The empty streets,
And blows the leaves,
Across the sweets.

When all are gone,
You're left to think,
Did they deserve,
To leave in blinks.

Words to Wall

We talk and text,
About our lives,
But mine don't hit,
The busy hive.

Maybe it's dead,
My words don't fit,
The empty slots,
And fall to pits.

Acts

Why questions form,
About your love,
When there's no proof,
To hold above.

Sometimes I wish,
You'd say it more,
But I see the acts,
From your core.

Blind

A fear consumes,
The way you think,
Making you blind,
Making you sink.

A light shines through,
To find the way,
Against the tide,
Of falling hay.

Lead Poisoning

Some people act,
As toddlers do,
When their age,
Is passed 42.

We must coddle,
And fake our way,
Just for a piece,
Of another day.

But then I know,
They're close in tow,
To Death's sweet door,
Forever more.

Saying No

Sometimes you jump,
With hopes in mind,
But where does life,
Leave you blind?

This and that,
They fill the hole,
Until you find,
Your perfect role.

Self-Respect

It's sad to see,
What people take,
From day to day,
Just for some cake.

And then you see,
The ones who snap,
Then Uppers wonder,
Who hid the cap.

Void

They suck you in,
To blindly watch,
Behind the screen,
Another notch.

The noose is set,
They say to go,
Just one more step,
Into the flow.

And blindly go,
Into the void,
Of questions sought,
And those you've toyed.

Mirror

Who sees your face,
When masks are down,
When you shine through,
As thoughts do crown.

You think you see,
Yourself in tow,
But who are you,
Without the show?

Useless

They wonder why,
We quit in droves,
When all they do,
Is feed the loaves.

They do not care,
What patients do,
So now we're off,
To something new.

Over Max

A moment comes,
When you must ask,
Why are you here?
And leave the mask.

Why go at 100,
And not 85?
You need your time,
To be alive.

Furlough

With nothing left,
But mind and time,
Do you sleep?
Or do you rhyme?

With nothing else,
No job or bills,
Do you lie flat?
Or live like new?

Wrinkles

Wrinkles form,
The time we see,
Along your face,
And by the sea.

But who you choose,
To see you through,
Will help you be,
The better you.

In the Closet

Some fear the world.
Some fear themselves.
But do you fear,
What's on the shelves?

They twitch and cry,
Sometimes you'll find,
Although their box,
Will not wind.

Father

I only wish,
That you could see,
The man I am,
Against the sea.

Years have passed,
Without a word,
So now your face,
Has nothing stirred.

I hope your life,
Is worth the loss,
Of those you push,
And those you toss.

www.ingramcontent.com/pod-product-compliance
Lightning Source LLC
Chambersburg PA
CBHW070736160726
48003CB00006BA/2532